# LET'S READ ABOUT INSECTS

# ANTS

by Susan Ashley

Reading consultant: Susan Nations, M.Ed., author/literacy coach/consultant

**WEEKLY READER®**

PUBLISHING

Please visit our web site at: www.weeklyreader.com.com
For a free catalog describing our list of high-quality books, call 1-800-542-2595 (USA)
or 1-800-387-3178 (Canada). Our fax: 1-877-542-2596.

**Library of Congress Cataloging-in-Publication Data.**

ISBN:978-1-60626-013-5(paperback).

This edition published especially for Books are Fun, a Reader's Digest Company.

Copyright © 2004 by
**Weekly Reader® Books**
An Imprint of Gareth Stevens Publishing
1 Reader's Digest Road
Plesantville, NY 10570-7000 USA

Editor: JoAnn Early Macken
Picture research: Diane Laska-Swanke
Art direction and page layout: Tammy West

Picture credits:  Cover © Kjell Sandved/Visuals Unlimited; title, p. 13 © Scott Camazine;
pp. 5, 7, 15, 21 © Robert & Linda Mitchell; p. 9 © George Loun/Visuals Unlimited;
p. 11 Tammy Gruenewald/© Weekly Reader Early Learning Library, 2004; pp. 17, 19
© James P. Rowan

Printed in China.

1 2 3 4 5 6 7 8 9 10 09 08

## Note to Educators and Parents

Reading is such an exciting adventure for young children! They are beginning to integrate their oral language skills with written language. To encourage children along the path to early literacy, books must be colorful, engaging, and interesting; they should invite the young reader to explore both the print and the pictures.

*Let's Read About Insects* is a new series designed to help children read about insect characteristics, life cycles, and communities. In each book, young readers will learn interesting facts about the featured insects and how they live.

Each book is specially designed to support the young reader in the reading process. The familiar topics are appealing to young children and invite them to read — and reread — again and again. The full-color photographs and enhanced text further support the student during the reading process.

In addition to serving as wonderful picture books in schools, libraries, homes, and other places where children learn to love reading, these books are specifically intended to be read within an instructional guided reading group. This small group setting allows beginning readers to work with a fluent adult model as they make meaning from the text. After children develop fluency with the text and content, the book can be read independently. Children and adults alike will find these books supportive, engaging, and fun!

— Susan Nations, M.Ed., author, literacy coach, and consultant in literacy development

Ants are social insects. They live in communities, just like people do. An ant community is called a **colony**. The ants in a colony live and work together.

5

Male ants, a queen ant, and workers live in a colony. Male ants mate with the queen and soon die. The queen spends all her time laying eggs.

queen

Most of the ants in a colony are workers. Workers are female ants. They gather food. They guard the colony from enemies. They work together to raise the young.

Workers build the colony's home. The home is called a **nest**. Workers dig in the soil with their legs. They carve out hundreds of rooms. Tunnels connect the rooms.

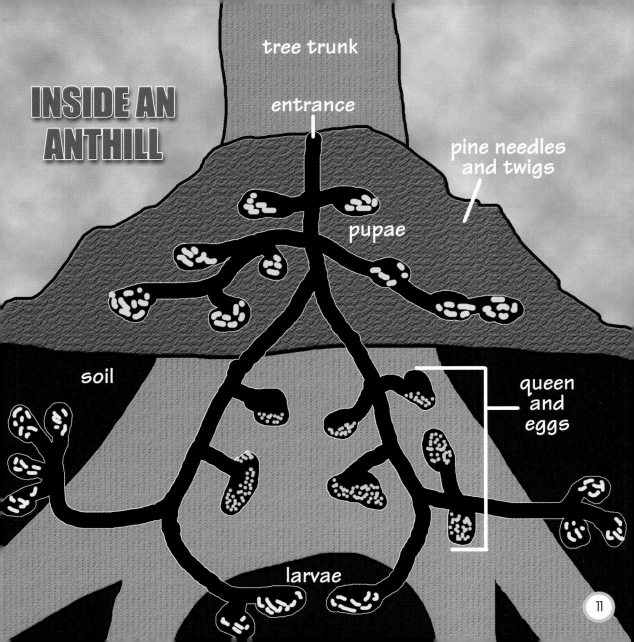

The queen lays her eggs in one of the rooms. Wormlike larvae hatch from the eggs. Workers clean and feed the larvae in special rooms.

After a few weeks, the larvae stop eating. They turn into pupae. Some types of pupae wrap up in silk cocoons. Soon the pupae turn into fully grown ants.

pupae

larvae

Like all insects, ants have six legs. Ants have two claws on the end of each leg. With their claws, ants can climb up walls. They can even walk upside down!

The two antennae on an ant's head always keep moving.  Ants use their antennae to taste, touch, and smell.  Ants use their antennae to find food.

Ants may be small, but they are very strong. An ant can lift an object that is twenty times its own weight!

# Glossary

**antennae** — feelers on the head of an insect or animal

**cocoons** — silk coverings some insects spin to protect themselves in the pupa stage

**larvae** — the wormlike second stage of growth of some insects

**pupae** — the third stage of growth of some insects

**social** — living with others in organized communities

# For More Information

## Books

Dorros, Arthur. Ant Cities. New York: HarperCollins, 1998.

Fowler, Allan. Inside an Ant Colony. Danbury, Conn.: Children's Press, 1998.

Hartley, Karen. Ant. Chicago: Heinemann Library, 2001.

Vaughan, Jenny. Ants. Milwaukee: Gareth Stevens, 1997.

## Web Site

## Enchanted Learning

www.ZoomSchool.com/subjects/ insects/ant/

Ant facts and printouts

# Index

# About the Author

**Susan Ashley** has written over eighteen books for children, including two picture books about dogs, Puppy Love and When I'm Happy, I Smile. She enjoys animals and writing about them. Susan lives in Wisconsin with her husband and two frisky felines.